THE LITTLE
DRUMMER BOY

THE LITTLE

DRUMMER BOY

Ezra Jack Keats

Words and Music by Katherine Davis,
Henry Onorati and Harry Simeone

The Bodley Head

LONDON SYDNEY TORONTO

ISBN 0 370 01511 8
Printed in Great Britain for The Bodley Head Ltd
9 Bow Street, London WC2E 7AL
by William Clowes and Sons Ltd, London and Beccles
First published by The Macmillan Company, New York, 1968
First published in Great Britain 1969
Reprinted 1973

Come, they told me,
(pa-rum-pum-pum-pum)

Our newborn King to see,
(pa-rum-pum-pum-pum)

Our finest gifts to bring
(pa-rum-pum-pum-pum)

To lay before the King,
(pa-rum-pum-pum-pum, rum-pum-pum-pum, rum-pum-pum-pum)

So to honour Him
(pa-rum-pum-pum-pum)

When we come.

Baby Jesus,
(pa-rum-pum-pum-pum)

I am a poor boy too,
(pa-rum-pum-pum-pum)

I have no gift to bring
(pa-rum-pum-pum-pum)

That's fit to give a king,
(pa-rum-pum-pum-pum,
rum-pum-pum-pum,
rum-pum-pum-pum)

Shall I play for you
(pa-rum-pum-pum-pum)

On my drum?

Mary nodded,
(pa-rum-pum-pum-pum)

The ox and lamb kept time,
(pa-rum-pum-pum-pum)

I played my drum for Him,
(pa-rum-pum-pum-pum)

I played my best for Him,
(pa-rum-pum-pum-pum,
rum-pum-pum-pum,
rum-pum-pum-pum)

Then He smiled at me,
(*pa-rum-pum-pum-pum*)

Me and my drum.

The Little Drummer Boy

Words and Music by KATHERINE DAVIS, HENRY ONORATI and HARRY SIMEONE

MODERATO

Come, they told me, pa-rum pum pum pum — Our new-born

King to see, pa-rum pum pum pum — Our fin-est gifts to bring, pa-

rum pum pum pum — To lay be-fore the King, pa-rum pum pum pum,

rum pum pum pum, rum pum pum pum — So to hon-our Him, pa-

rum pum pum pum — When — we come. —

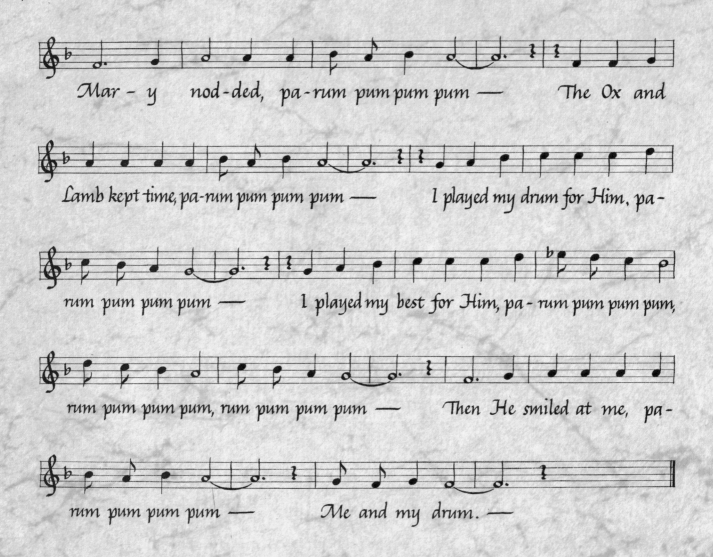

Mar – y nod-ded, pa-rum pum pum pum — The Ox and

Lamb kept time, pa-rum pum pum pum — I played my drum for Him, pa-

rum pum pum pum — I played my best for Him, pa-rum pum pum pum,

rum pum pum pum, rum pum pum pum — Then He smiled at me, pa-

rum pum pum pum — Me and my drum. —